PEOPLE AT THE CENTER OF

WATERGATE

By ROB EDELMAN

BLACKBIRCH PRESS
An imprint of Thomson Gale, a part of The Thomson Corporation

Detroit • New York • San Francisco • San Diego • New Haven, Conn. • Waterville, Maine • London • Munich

© 2005 Thomson Gale, a part of The Thomson Corporation.

Thomson and Star Logo are trademarks and Gale and Blackbirch Press are registered trademarks used herein under license.

For more information, contact
Blackbirch Press
27500 Drake Rd.
Farmington Hills, MI 48331-3535
Or you can visit our Internet site at http://www.gale.com

ALL RIGHTS RESERVED.
No part of this work covered by the copyright hereon may be reproduced or used in any form or by any means—graphic, electronic, or mechanical, including photocopying, recording, taping, Web distribution, or information storage retrieval systems—without the written permission of the publisher.

Every effort has been made to trace the owners of copyrighted material.

Picture credits: cover: center © ChromoSohm, Inc./CORBIS; top left and right © Wally McNamee/CORBIS; bottom left, center, and right © Bettmann/CORBIS. Pages 8, 11, 19, 20, 30, 33 © AP/Wide World Photos; pages 6–7, 12, 13, 15, 16, 17, 18, 22–23, 24, 26, 27, 29, 31, 32, 35, 39, 40, 41 © Bettmann/CORBIS; page 10 © Dennis Brack/Landov; pages 21, 28 © CORBIS; page 9 © Owen Franken/CORBIS; page 5 © Todd A. Gipstein/CORBIS; page 14 © Robert Maass/CORBIS; pages 43 © Wally McNamee/CORBIS; page 36 © Jules Perrier/CORBIS.

LIBRARY OF CONGRESS CATALOGING-IN-PUBLICATION DATA

Edelman, Rob.
  Watergate / by Rob Edelman.
    p. cm. — (People at the center of)
  Includes bibliographical references and index.
  ISBN 1-56711-928-X (alk. paper)
  1. Watergate Affair, 1972–1974—Juvenile literature. 2. Nixon, Richard M. (Richard Milhous), 1913–Juvenile literature. 3. Nixon, Richard M. (Richard Milhous), 1913– Friends and associates—Juvenile literature. I. Title. II. Series.

E860.E315 2005
973.924—dc22

2004014012

Printed in the United States of America

Contents

Introduction 4
Frank Wills 10
E. Howard Hunt 12
G. Gordon Liddy 14
James W. McCord Jr. 16
John J. Sirica 18
Richard M. Nixon 20
John Mitchell 24
H.R. "Bob" Haldeman 26
John D. Ehrlichman 28
Rose Mary Woods 30
John W. Dean III 32
Bob Woodward and Carl Bernstein 34
"Deep Throat" 36
Archibald Cox 38
Sam J. Ervin Jr. 40
Peter W. Rodino Jr. 42
Chronology 44
For Further Information 46
Index 47
About the Author 48

PEOPLE AT THE CENTER OF

WATERGATE

Watergate was a political scandal that seized the attention of the American public during the early 1970s and culminated in the resignation of a U.S. president. The affair began on June 17, 1972, when Richard Nixon, a Republican who had become America's thirty-seventh chief executive in 1968, was preparing his reelection campaign. Early that morning, five members of the "plumbers" (a top secret organization authorized by Nixon's White House to stop news leaks to the media) broke into the Democratic National Committee headquarters, located in the Watergate office complex in Washington, D.C. Their intention was to plant a hidden listening device, allowing them to eavesdrop on conversations involving Democratic strategists. Before they could complete their mission, they were arrested.

One of the intruders, James W. McCord Jr., was security director of the Committee for the Reelection of the President (CREEP), a White House–founded fundraising group. Two days after the break-in, John Mitchell, Nixon's former attorney general and the head of CREEP, claimed to have no knowledge of the operation. Then in August 1972, the *Washington Post* reported that a twenty-five-thousand-dollar CREEP donation had been deposited in the bank account of Bernard L. Barker, another Watergate burglar. The following month, the *Post* reported that, when he was attorney general, Mitchell managed a top secret fund used by the Republicans to spy on Democratic political activity.

By October 1972, the Federal Bureau of Investigation (FBI) had uncovered sufficient evidence to link the Watergate break-in to Nixon's reelection campaign. Even so, on November 7, Nixon was swept back into office in a landslide over his Democratic opponent, South Dakota senator George McGovern.

On January 30, 1973, scant days after the beginning of Nixon's second term, McCord and G. Gordon Liddy, former finance counsel for CREEP, were convicted

Members of a secret group linked to the Nixon White House broke into the Democratic National Committee's office at the Watergate complex (above) to bug the telephones.

of conspiracy, burglary, and wiretapping. Although he had not actually participated in the break-in, Liddy helped to plan it. On April 30, Nixon delivered a speech in which he stated that he was distressed to learn that CREEP employees had been implicated in the break-in but remained convinced that no one in his administration had been involved.

On May 18, 1973, the U.S. Senate Select Committee to Investigate Campaign Practices began its Watergate hearings. A significant piece of damning evidence against Nixon came on June 3, when John Dean, his former legal counsel, reported to the committee that he had discussed with the president a Watergate cover-up (a White House effort to hinder the investigation) on over thirty-five occasions. On July 13, Alexander Butterfield, the president's former appointments secretary, testified that Nixon had been making audiotape recordings of his Oval Office conversations since 1971. Archibald Cox, the U.S. Justice Department's special prosecutor for Watergate, subpoenaed the White House for all Watergate-related recordings

and documents. The president refused to surrender them. On August 15, he told the American people that discussions between a U.S. president and his advisers needed to be kept confidential as a matter of national security.

Cox still insisted on receiving all the material. He was fired by the president on October 20, at which time Elliot Richardson, the U.S. attorney general, and his deputy, William D. Ruckelshaus, quit in protest. Talk of impeachment (the procedure in which a president is removed from office by a majority vote of the House of Representatives and a two-thirds vote by the Senate) began to swell within the ranks of

The Senate Select Committee to Investigate Campaign Practices listens to testimony during the Watergate hearings in July 1973.

Congress and among the public. Nixon finally agreed to release some—but not all—of the audiotapes. Still, suspicions were aroused further when the White House could not account for an eighteen-and-a-half-minute gap on one of the tapes.

On February 6, 1974, the Committee on the Judiciary of the House of Representatives was authorized to determine if Nixon's actions warranted impeachment. The committee wished to review additional Oval Office andiotapes and issued a subpoena for them on April 11. In response, the White House made available over twelve hundred pages of Nixon auditotape transcripts. They were, however, edited. The committee demanded the actual audiotapes and issued three additional subpoenas.

In July 1974, the U.S. Supreme Court unanimously ruled that the president must release the audiotapes. He did so—and one of them was the infamous smoking gun recording, which offered evidence that Nixon had been involved in the Watergate

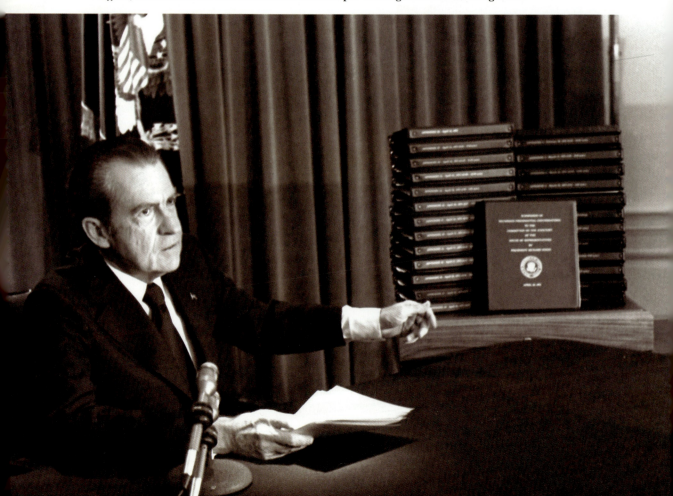

President Richard M. Nixon, pointing to transcripts of taped conversations in the Oval Office, announces he will release the transcripts to congressional investigators.

Women at a Washington airport read about Nixon, the only U.S. president to resign from office.

cover-up as early as June 23, 1972. On the tape, Nixon was heard conferring with White House chief of staff H.R. Haldeman over a strategy that involved having the Central Intelligence Agency (CIA) advise the FBI not to participate in the break-in investigation because the nation's security was at risk.

On July 27, the House committee adopted Article 1 of the impeachment resolution, which charged Nixon with obstructing the Watergate break-in investigation. On July 29, the committee adopted Article II, which charged the president with misusing his powers and violating his oath of office. That same day, the committee adopted Article III, which charged the president with failing to submit to the House subpoenas. The voting extended beyond political party lines, as some Republicans joined Democrats in advocating impeachment.

On the evening of August 8, 1974, in a nationally televised speech, Richard Nixon resigned from the office of the presidency. The following morning, he submitted a resignation letter to Henry Kissinger, his secretary of state, and was replaced by Gerald Ford, his vice president.

Many of those involved in the Watergate affair, including members of Nixon's White House staff, served jail sentences. Nixon, however, evaded going to prison. On September 8, 1974, he was pardoned by Gerald Ford for all wrongdoing.

Frank Wills

Discovered the Watergate burglary in progress

Frank Wills was born in Savannah, Georgia, in 1947. He and his mother moved to North Augusta in 1958, and he came to Washington, D.C., in 1971.

Upon settling in the nation's capital, Wills was hired as a security guard by GSS, a security services company. His salary was eighty dollars per week, and his assignment was to work the midnight to 7:00 A.M. shift at the Watergate office complex. At approximately 1:00 A.M. on the night of June 17, 1972, Wills was making his rounds through the buildings. He observed that adhesive tape had been placed over part of the lock on a door located between a stairway and a basement garage. The positioning of the tape kept the door unlocked. Wills assumed that the Watergate cleaning staff had taped over the lock. He removed the tape and continued his rounds.

A bit later, as he went past the same door, Wills noticed that a new piece of tape had been placed over the lock. His suspicions were aroused because he knew that the janitorial workers had left for the night. Wills telephoned the Washington, D.C., police department. Three plainclothes officers were dispatched to the scene. At 2:30 A.M. they apprehended five men who were in the process of bugging the Democratic National Committee offices, located on the complex's sixth floor. Had it not been for Wills's watchfulness, the Watergate scandal might never have transpired.

When Watergate security guard Frank Wills noticed that a door lock in the Watergate office complex had been tampered with, he became suspicious and called police.

Wills left GSS in 1973. Once the significance of the burglary was evident, he became a minor celebrity. He was interviewed by journalists. He hired an agent. He appeared as himself in *All the President's Men*, the 1976 film version of the best-selling account of the break-in and its aftermath.

After the media spotlight faded, Wills had difficulty securing full-time employment. In the late 1970s, he moved in with his mother. In 1983, he was sentenced to prison for a year for stealing a twelve-dollar pair of sneakers. He was destitute when he died of a brain tumor in 2000.

E. Howard Hunt

Helped plan the Watergate break-in

Everette Howard Hunt was born in East Hamburg, New York, in 1918. During World War II (1939–1945), he was a member of the Office of Strategic Services (OSS), which gathered and analyzed information and spearheaded acts of sabotage and espionage against America's enemies. In 1949, he became an agent with the CIA, which replaced the OSS. He primarily was stationed in Mexico and Guatemala.

Hunt retired from the CIA in 1970, and his agency experience made him suitable for recruitment as a White House security adviser. After coming to the Oval Office, Hunt became a member of the White House Special Investigations Unit, also known as the "plumbers": a top secret group whose purpose was to halt government leaks to the media.

Hunt and fellow plumber G. Gordon Liddy planned the bugging of the Democratic National Committee headquarters on June 17, 1972. He was connected to the break-in when his phone number was discovered in the address books of several burglars. This finding was one of the first connections between the break-in and the White House. On September 15, Hunt and six others—Liddy, Bernard L. Barker, James W. McCord Jr., Virgilio Gonzalez, Eugenio Martinez, and Frank Sturgis—were indicted for their participation in the break-in. Their trial began on January 8, 1973. Three days later, Hunt pleaded guilty to charges of conspiracy, burglary, and wiretapping. He was fined ten thousand dollars and spent thirty-three months in prison.

Hunt eventually settled in Florida and in 1995 filed for bankruptcy. He has published several dozen spy novels and thrillers.

Some of the "plumbers" accused in the Watergate break-in walk to court (above). White House security adviser E. Howard Hunt (right) masterminded the break-in with G. Gordon Liddy.

G. Gordon Liddy

Helped plan the Watergate break-in

George Gordon Battle Liddy was born in 1930 in Hoboken, New Jersey. He graduated from Fordham University in New York in 1952, served in the U.S. Army, and completed a law degree at Fordham in 1957. That year, he became an FBI agent. He left the FBI in 1962 and began his law career, working for himself and then as a New York State prosecutor.

After working on Richard Nixon's successful 1968 presidential campaign, Liddy was hired as a U.S. Treasury Department lawyer. In 1971, he joined Nixon's White House staff. He became a member of the White House Special Investigations Unit, also known as the "plumbers." The following year, he was named finance counsel for CREEP.

Liddy concocted a scheme, called Operation Gemstone, which he submitted to John Mitchell, Nixon's former attorney general and the head of CREEP. The plan called for spying on and discrediting the president's political opponents and kidnapping potential 1972 Republican National Convention protesters. Due to its cost, Mitchell rejected Operation Gemstone. He did, however, authorize Liddy to set in motion a scaled-back version. This evolved into the Watergate break-in, the specifics of which were planned by Liddy and fellow plumber E. Howard Hunt.

G. Gordon Liddy (second from left) is escorted by federal officers to the Los Angeles County jail. Liddy plotted the Watergate office break-in with E. Howard Hunt.

In January 1973, Liddy was convicted of conspiracy, burglary, and wiretapping in connection with Watergate. He was sentenced to a twenty-year prison term, of which he served four and a half years. President Jimmy Carter commuted his sentence in 1977, based on the fact that no other Watergate conspirator had spent that much time in jail.

Liddy published his autobiography in 1980. He then appeared as a panelist on television game shows, guest starred and played himself in movies and action-adventure television series, gave lectures across the country, and authored novels and books on politics. In 1992, he began a career as a conservative radio talk show host.

JAMES W. MCCORD JR.

PARTICIPATED IN THE WATERGATE BREAK-IN

James Walter McCord Jr. was born in Waurika, Oklahoma, in 1918. He attended Baylor University in Texas and served in the U.S. military during World War II. He joined the FBI in 1948 and three years later was hired by the CIA, where he became chief of security at the agency's Langley, Virginia, compound. He left the CIA in 1970.

McCord established a private security firm, McCord Associates, which was employed by the Republican National Committee. On January 1, 1972, he became security director of CREEP. He also was one of the five participants in the Watergate break-in. It was McCord who placed, and then replaced, the adhesive tape over part of the lock on the Watergate stairway door. Had he not done so, the break-in might have gone undiscovered.

When McCord and his cronies were arrested, all were wearing surgical gloves and were carrying lock picks and door jimmies (small crowbars). They had a walkie-talkie, a shortwave radio, 35-millimeter still-photograph cameras, unexposed film, and equipment for picking up and transmitting conversations. McCord's CREEP affiliation, reported two days later in the *Washington Post*, was the first public link between the Watergate burglary and the White House.

McCord and his cohorts went on trial in January 1973. All but McCord and G. Gordon Liddy pled guilty; both were convicted of conspiracy, burglary, and wiretapping. McCord then wrote a letter to John Sirica, the presiding judge, in which he claimed that the Watergate defendants who admitted guilt did so under pressure from the White House, which had been aware of the burglary and was trying to cover it up. He added that John Dean, the president's legal counsel, and John Mitchell, the head of CREEP, pressured him to lie on the witness stand. These accusations triggered Watergate investigators to seek additional evidence connecting the break-in to the Oval Office.

McCord served four months in jail for taking part in the burglary. He also authored a book, published in 1974 and titled *A Piece of Tape—The Watergate Story: Fact and Fiction*. He eventually settled in Fort Collins, Colorado, where he operated a solar-energy company.

James W. McCord Jr. shows the telephone listening device planted in the Democratic National Committee's office during the break-in.

18 WATERGATE

John J. Sirica

Judge who presided over the Watergate trials

John Joseph Sirica was born in Waterbury, Connecticut, in 1904. He graduated from Georgetown University Law School in Washington, D.C., in 1926, and for the next three decades worked as a criminal lawyer. In 1957, as a reward for his years of service to the Republican Party, he won a federal judgeship. He was assigned to the U.S. District Court for the District of Columbia.

By 1973, Sirica had become the court's chief justice. In this capacity, he presided over the trials of those accused in the Watergate break-in. He was determined to learn the truth behind the burglary and on occasion personally questioned witnesses, an unorthodox procedure for a judge. He told jurors to reflect not only on the events that occurred but on why they occurred, and he spoke up when he felt witnesses were not being truthful. After the trial, Sirica released a letter written to him by James W. McCord Jr., one of the defendants. In the letter, McCord claimed that White House staff members pressured the Watergate defendants to plead guilty and lie while under oath.

When President Richard Nixon refused to hand over to Watergate investigators the audiotapes of his Oval Office conversations, citing the concept of executive privilege (the legal principle that conversations between a president and his advisers be kept confidential because of national security), Sirica ordered him to do so. This ruling pitted the judicial and executive branches of government against each other. On July 24, 1974, the U.S. Supreme Court unanimously ruled in favor of Sirica and ordered Nixon to release all the requested audiotapes. The president resigned from office two weeks later. Sirica then presided over the trials of additional Watergate conspirators.

Sirica wrote about Watergate in a 1979 book titled *To Set the Record Straight*. He offered the opinion that Nixon should have been indicted for his participation in the affair. Sirica retired in 1986 and died of a heart attack in 1992.

John J. Sirica pushed for truthfulness in the Watergate trials. At right are audiotapes Nixon withheld during the investigation.

Richard M. Nixon

U.S. president and central figure in the Watergate scandal

Richard Milhous Nixon was born in Yorba Linda, California, in 1913. He graduated from Whittier College and Duke University Law School, served in the U.S. Navy during World War II, and was elected to the U.S. House of Representatives in 1946 and the Senate in 1950. Nixon was vice president between 1952 and 1960, but he lost the 1960 presidential election and the 1962 California gubernatorial race. Despite these defeats, he won the presidency in 1968 and ran for reelection in 1972.

Nixon trounced his Democratic rival, George McGovern, and began his second term in January 1973. As the Watergate break-in increasingly was being reported in the media, the president emerged as the scandal's central figure. Rumors swirled with regard to his knowledge of the burglary and its subsequent cover-up.

Richard M. Nixon answers questions from the press about Watergate. When the audiotapes proved Nixon was behind the cover-up, he resigned rather than face impeachment.

On April 30, 1973, Nixon delivered a speech in which he expressed his alarm over the break-in and dismay upon learning of the participation of CREEP employees. He also conveyed his belief that no White House staff person took part. Yet Nixon's own Watergate involvement remained in question. Although that uncertainty could have been clarified with the release of secret audiotape recordings that he had been making since 1971, the president refused to hand over this evidence to Watergate investigators, citing executive privilege.

The U.S. Supreme Court eventually ruled that all tapes be made available. One was the infamous smoking gun recording, which offered proof that Nixon had been involved in the Watergate cover-up as early as June 23, 1972. During the summer of 1974, the Committee on the Judiciary of the House of Representatives voted to consent to three of four proposed articles of impeachment against the president. Before impeachment proceedings began, Nixon resigned on August 8. He was replaced by Gerald Ford, his vice president.

After leaving office, Nixon wrote books and gave speeches on American foreign policy. His supporters regarded him as a beloved elder statesman, while his opponents condemned him for lengthening the Vietnam War (1941–1975) and lying to the American public during the Watergate investigation. He died of a massive stroke in New York City in 1994.

After resigning as president, Nixon pauses to give the "victory" sign as he boards a White House helicopter.

John Mitchell
Watergate coconspirator

John Newton Mitchell was born in Detroit, Michigan, in 1913. He attended New York's Fordham University Law School and began his law career in 1938. He became a partner in the Manhattan law firm of Caldwell and Raymond in 1942, served in the U.S. Navy during World War II, and then returned to his legal practice.

In 1967, Mitchell's and Richard Nixon's law firms merged. The two men became close friends, and Mitchell managed Nixon's 1968 presidential campaign. The newly elected chief executive named Mitchell his attorney general. He immediately earned headlines for his vocal condemnation of Vietnam War protesters and advocated such controversial policies as using wiretaps without court orders and setting up private detention facilities for alleged criminals.

In 1972, Mitchell resigned his position as attorney general to take charge of CREEP. Two days after the June 17, 1972, Watergate break-in, the *Washington Post* reported that James W. McCord Jr., the CREEP security director, was one of the burglars. Mitchell told the *Post* that those arrested were not acting on behalf of the reelection committee.

Mitchell did, however, resign from CREEP on July 1. Then on September 29 the *Post* reported that he had managed a top secret fund employed by the Republicans to spy on Democratic political activity. Jeb Stuart Magruder, a former CREEP assistant, and John Dean, the former White House counsel, eventually testified before the Senate Select Committee to Investigate Campaign Practices that Mitchell agreed to spend $250,000 to finance the Watergate burglary.

Of all those implicated in the Watergate scandal, Mitchell remained the most fiercely loyal to Nixon. He testified before the committee that he was aware of the Watergate cover-up, but he offered a minimum amount of information during his three-day interrogation. He declared that the reelection of his president was his primary concern and took priority over all else.

In 1974, Mitchell went on trial for his Watergate involvement. On January 1, 1975, he was convicted of obstruction of justice, conspiracy, and perjury. He spent nineteen months in prison and died in 1988.

John Mitchell, former attorney general and director of Nixon's reelection campaign, stayed deeply loyal to his friend Richard Nixon.

H.R. "Bob" Haldeman

Watergate coconspirator

Harry Robbins "Bob" Haldeman was born in Los Angeles in 1926. After serving in the U.S. Naval Reserve during World War II, he graduated from the University of California at Los Angeles in 1948. He then was hired by the J. Walter Thompson advertising agency, and in 1959 he became vice president and manager of the company's California headquarters. Long a Richard Nixon supporter, he was chief of staff of Nixon's successful 1968 presidential campaign.

After the election, Haldeman became the new president's White House chief of staff. He quickly won a reputation as a well-organized office manager and fiercely loyal caretaker of Nixon. He became one of the president's closest advisers and grew to be regarded as the second most powerful person in the country.

H.R. "Bob" Haldeman receives advice from his attorney (above). Haldeman served as Nixon's chief of staff and became one of his closest advisers.

Haldeman fostered the win-at-all-costs mentality that led to the White House endorsing the Watergate break-in. He also was involved in the Watergate cover-up from its earliest stages. He had been in conversation with the president during the notorious eighteen-and-a-half-minute gap on an audiotape Nixon made in the White House on June 20, 1972, three days after the break-in. He had been talking with Nixon on the "smoking gun" recording, made on June 23, that implicated the president in the cover-up.

The escalating scandal led to Haldeman's resignation on April 30, 1973. For his Watergate involvement, he was convicted of conspiracy and obstruction of justice in 1974 and spent eighteen months in prison. In his 1978 book *The Ends of Power*, he accepted blame for creating an environment in the White House that allowed Watergate to come about.

Afterward, Haldeman became vice president of a real estate firm. He died of cancer in 1993. The following year, his Watergate memoir, titled *The Haldeman Diaries*, was published.

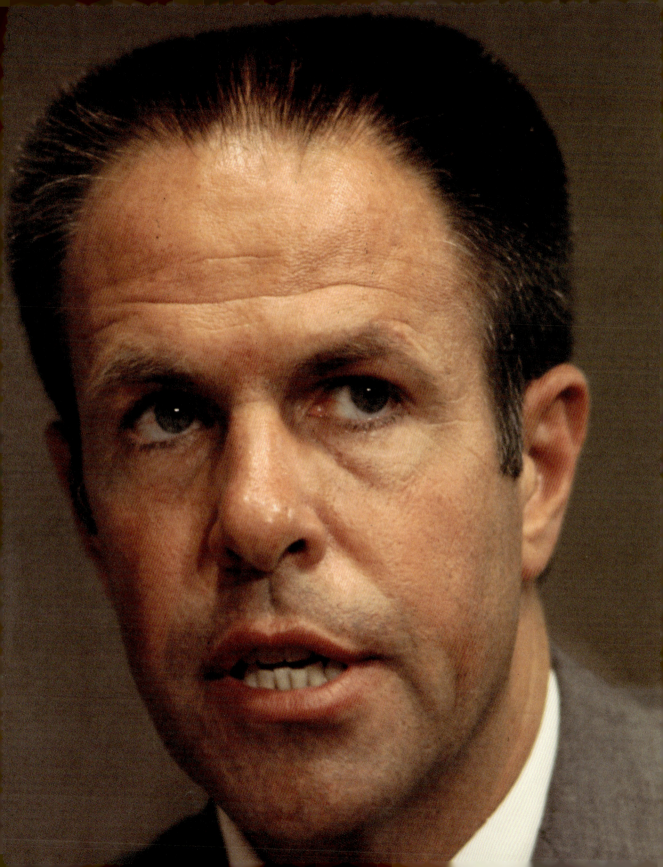

John D. Ehrlichman

Head of the White House "plumbers"

John Daniel Ehrlichman was born in Tacoma, Washington, in 1925. He served in the U.S. Army Air Force during World War II, graduated from the University of California at Los Angeles in 1948 and Stanford University School of Law in 1951, and then was employed by a Seattle law firm.

Ehrlichman worked on Richard Nixon's campaign staff during Nixon's unsuccessful 1960 presidential bid. After his 1968 election, Nixon first named Ehrlichman presidential counsel and then White House assistant for domestic affairs. Ehrlichman's job was to offer advice on national issues, but his central task became overseeing the administration's offensive against the Democratic Party, the anti–Vietnam War movement, and any and all Nixon political rivals.

In 1971, Ehrlichman established the White House "plumbers," the top secret group whose attempt to break into and bug the Democratic National Committee headquarters sparked the Watergate affair. During this period, he and Nixon also discussed employing the Internal Revenue Service (IRS) to examine the taxes of political adversaries.

After the Watergate break-in, Ehrlichman disbanded the plumbers. Because of his close involvement with the group, he was ordered by Nixon to distance himself from the cover-up. As the Watergate controversy escalated, he resigned his post on April 30, 1973. During his 1974 trial, he was convicted of conspiracy, obstruction of justice, and perjury during the Watergate investigation. He served eighteen months in prison.

After his release, Ehrlichman became a television and radio commentator and worked for an engineering consulting firm. He wrote several novels along with two Watergate memoirs, *The Whole Truth* and *Witness to Power: The Nixon Years*. He died of complications from diabetes in 1999.

John D. Ehrlichman organized the group that broke into the Democratic National Committee headquarters. Above, he swears to tell the truth to the Senate Watergate committee.

Rose Mary Woods

Richard Nixon's private secretary

Rose Mary Woods was born in Sebring, Ohio, in 1917. She settled in Washington, D.C., in 1943 and became a secretary for a special U.S. House of Representatives committee. In 1951, Richard Nixon, then a U.S. senator, hired her as his private secretary.

In November 1973, the Senate Select Committee to Investigate Campaign Practices made it known that a gap existed on an audiotape that Nixon had recorded. It was labeled "Watergate tape 342" and was made on June 20, 1972, three days after the Watergate break-in. The recording consisted of an Oval Office discussion between Nixon and H.R. Haldeman, his chief of staff. At one point, their conversation faded away. For the next eighteen and a half minutes, it was replaced by hisses, hums, and clicks. The committee insisted that the president explain the reason for the gap.

Rose Mary Woods demonstrates how she might have accidentally erased part of an audiotape while answering the phone. Woods worked as Nixon's secretary from the time he was a senator.

Woods testified that the erasure was her fault. As she transcribed the audiotape, she explained, her telephone rang. When she stretched behind to reach for the phone, she accidentally pushed the tape recorder's record (rather than stop) button. Her foot also remained on the recorder's operating pedal. As a result, the tape was erased. When she was asked to reenact the incident, Woods pantomimed her movements. She added that the gap she caused could not have been longer than five minutes, which was the length of the phone call.

At the time, Nixon's trustworthiness in the eyes of the American public was rapidly diminishing. The disclosure of the gap and Woods's testimony gave evidence of further ineptitude on the part of Nixon and his staff and suggested that the president was concealing incriminating information from Watergate investigators.

After Nixon resigned the presidency on August 9, 1974, he and his family flew to their home in San Clemente, California. Woods accompanied them. The former president valued her loyalty, and she continued working for him until 1976. Then she retired and settled in Alliance, Ohio.

John W. Dean III

Testified about Nixon's involvement in the cover-up

John Wesley Dean III was born in Akron, Ohio, in 1938. He graduated from the College of Wooster in Ohio in 1961 and Georgetown University in Washington, D.C., four years later. He then was named chief counsel to the Republican members of the Committee on the Judiciary of the House of Representatives. After Richard Nixon's 1968 presidential victory, Dean became U.S. associate attorney general. He then replaced John Ehrlichman as the counsel to the president.

After the Watergate break-in four years later, Nixon entrusted the cover-up to Dean. The president announced that the lawyer would head an investigation to unearth any clandestine Oval Office participation in the burglary and eventually reported that none could be found. On April 30, 1973, the president told the American public that the White House would not obstruct any Watergate inquiry. Dean, however, was fired on that date, because Nixon had learned that he was providing Watergate prosecutors with evidence involving the White House's connection to the burglary.

John W. Dean III testified at the Senate Select Committee hearings that Nixon participated in the Watergate cover-up.

In June, Dean testified before the Senate Select Committee to Investigate Campaign Practices that Nixon had been directly involved in an extensive amount of illegal activity. This included employing the FBI and IRS to pester Nixon's political opponents, involving the CIA in the Watergate cover-up, and giving hush money to Watergate burglars. Dean noted that he had discussed the cover-up with the president on over thirty-five occasions.

Nixon and his former aides strongly disputed Dean's testimony. It eventually was substantiated with the release of Nixon's White House audiotapes. Dean was convicted of obstruction of justice and spent four months in prison.

Dean published two Watergate memoirs, *Blind Ambition* and *Lost Honor*. He became an investment banker and authored articles on politics and law along with additional books. One of them, *Unmasking Deep Throat*, was published as an e-book in 2002.

Bob Woodward and Carl Bernstein

Reporters who investigated the Watergate break-in

Robert Upshur Woodward was born in Geneva, Illinois, in 1943. He attended Yale University, graduating in 1965, and served as a communications officer in the U.S. Navy from 1965 to 1970. He was hired by the *Washington Post* in 1971. Carl Bernstein was born in Washington, D.C., in 1944. He took classes at the University of Maryland and was hired by the *Post* in 1966.

When word came that five men had broken into the Democratic National Committee headquarters on the night of June 17, 1972, most newspapers across the country barely took notice. The break-in was reported, but not as a front-page story, and it was viewed by many editors as a minor news item, a bungled caper. Woodward and Bernstein, who then were obscure *Post* reporters, thought otherwise, and teamed to further investigate the attempted break-in.

On June 19, in an article headlined "GOP [Grand Old Party, or the Republican Party] Security Aide Among Five Arrested in Bugging Affair," Woodward and Bernstein were the first to link the burglars to CREEP. As the months passed, their investigation and subsequent news items connected the break-in to prominent Nixon administration officials, in addition to CREEP. They also reported on White House–instigated illegal activities such as theft, wiretapping, and attempts to disturb Democratic Party activities. They uncovered evidence of the manner in which the president employed the CIA and FBI to penalize his enemies. Their journalistic efforts helped transform Watergate from a minor newspaper story into a major media event.

For their efforts, Woodward and Bernstein earned the Pulitzer Prize in 1973. Their best-selling account of the scandal, *All the President's Men*, was published in 1974. It became an Academy Award–winning motion picture in 1976. That year, they coauthored *The Final Days*, a second Watergate-related book, which chronicled Nixon's last days in office.

Bernstein left the *Washington Post* in 1976 and since has held various high-status positions in the American media. Woodward became an assistant managing editor of the *Post* in 1979 and has authored numerous books on American and international politics.

Washington Post *reporters Bob Woodward (left) and Carl Bernstein (right) investigated the Watergate break-in and wrote the news stories that turned it into a major political scandal.*

 "Deep Throat"

Provided leads to investigative reporters

As *Washington Post* reporters Bob Woodward and Carl Bernstein investigated the events surrounding the Watergate break-in, one of their key contacts was an unidentified individual who came to be known as "Deep Throat." This person provided the journalists with critical leads and bits of information as they delved into the botched burglary and its subsequent cover-up.

In *All the President's Men*, their account of the scandal, Woodward and Bernstein confirmed that Deep Throat occupied an important post in the executive branch of the U.S. government. Deep Throat did not give the reporters incriminating evidence, but offered them suggestions and backed up or refuted information they uncovered. One such suggestion was that the reporters "follow the money," which led them to investigate contributions to Richard Nixon's reelection campaign.

Over the years, the identity of Deep Throat has been the source of much speculation. Woodward and Bernstein confirmed that the contact had access to the corridors of power in Washington, from the White House to the FBI, the U.S. Department of Justice to CREEP. The journalists, however, refused to divulge his identity.

In 1997, on the twenty-fifth anniversary of the Watergate break-in, Woodward declared that he had promised not to name Deep Throat unless the source chose to go public. Because he had not, the reporter was intent on keeping his vow.

Three years later, Bernstein noted that just three individuals—excluding Deep Throat himself—knew the identity of the secret contact. The trio to which he referred was himself, Woodward, and Ben Bradlee, formerly the executive editor of the *Washington Post* who supervised the reporters during their Watergate investigation.

The informant "Deep Throat" met secretly with Woodward and Bernstein, confirming or denying information they uncovered. They have never revealed Deep Throat's identity.

ARCHIBALD COX

SPECIAL PROSECUTOR WHO INVESTIGATED WATERGATE

Archibald Cox Jr. was born in Plainfield, New Jersey, in 1912. He graduated from Harvard University's law school in 1937 and began practicing his profession. After holding positions with the National Defense Board and Office of the Solicitor General during World War II, he became a full professor at Harvard. During the 1960s, he was solicitor general (the third-highest position in the U.S. Justice Department), serving during the presidential administrations of John Kennedy and Lyndon Johnson.

On May 18, 1973, U.S. attorney general–designate Elliot Richardson named Cox to the newly established post of the U.S. Justice Department's special prosecutor for Watergate. His assignment was to examine the facts surrounding the alleged Watergate cover-up and any other illegal goings-on during the 1972 presidential race. He was authorized to work independently and was given unprecedented power.

On July 13, Alexander Butterfield, Richard Nixon's former appointments secretary, disclosed that the president had been making audiotape recordings of his Oval Office discussions since 1971. Cox promptly subpoenaed the White House for all Watergate-related audiotapes. Nixon refused to hand them over, citing executive privilege.

The U.S. Court of Appeals rebuffed Nixon and ruled that executive privilege did not apply to these particular tapes. The president still declined to give Cox the material, offering only to submit written outlines of their content. When Cox found this an unacceptable compromise and insisted on receiving the original tapes, Nixon ordered Richardson to fire the special prosecutor. Richardson refused. On October 20, 1973, in what came to be known as the "Saturday Night Massacre," Nixon himself fired Cox. Richardson and the deputy attorney general, William D. Ruckelshaus, resigned in protest. Nonetheless, Cox's actions eventually led to Nixon being forced to turn over the tapes, which proved the president's involvement in the cover-up beyond a doubt.

After the Watergate affair, Cox worked with Common Cause, an organization that promotes the passage of ethics-related laws and changes in the manner in which political campaigns are financed. He also taught at Harvard and Boston University law schools. Cox died of old age in 2004.

Special prosecutor Archibald Cox demanded the original Watergate audiotapes from Nixon, who fired Cox as a result.

Sam J. Ervin Jr.

Led Senate committee that investigated Watergate

Samuel James Ervin Jr. was born in Morganton, North Carolina, in 1896. He graduated from the University of North Carolina in 1917, served in the U.S. military during World War I (1914–1918), and graduated from Harvard University's law school in 1922. He then became a lawyer in his hometown, was thrice elected to the North Carolina State Assembly, and between 1948 and 1954 was a state supreme court judge. He became a U.S. senator in 1954.

Ervin's firm belief that the U.S. Constitution rose above political philosophy led Mike Mansfield, the Senate majority leader, to select him to chair the Senate Select Committee to Investigate Campaign Practices, which probed the Watergate break-in. The committee began its hearings on May 18, 1973. Throughout the inquiry, Ervin presented himself as a sharp-minded, self-described "old country lawyer" who was intent upon distinguishing between what is ethical and what is criminal. His facial expressions indicated his ire over a great deal of the testimony.

Sam J. Ervin Jr. (second from left) served as chairman of the Senate Select Committee that investigated the Watergate affair.

As the hearings proceeded, Ervin became convinced that Richard Nixon and his underlings endorsed various schemes to undermine the Democratic Party's 1972 presidential campaign effort. He also believed that, after the Watergate break-in, they attempted to cover up their illegal actions. He tartly observed that the U.S. Constitution did not sanction the committing of criminal acts by U.S. presidents.

Ervin retired to his hometown in December 1974, four months after Nixon's resignation. He wrote several books and died in 1985 of respiratory failure while being treated for kidney failure.

Peter W. Rodino Jr.

Led committee that voted to impeach Nixon

Peter Wallace Rodino Jr. was born in Newark, New Jersey, in 1909. He earned a degree from the New Jersey School of Law (which eventually became Rutgers University) in 1937, practiced in his hometown, served in the U.S. Army during World War II, and was elected to the U.S. House of Representatives in 1948.

On February 6, 1974, the House authorized its Committee on the Judiciary to determine if adequate cause existed for it to employ its constitutional authority to impeach Richard Nixon. As committee chair, Rodino was charged with overseeing the hearings.

Rodino understood that, if the president were to be impeached, those on the committee needed to place Republican and Democratic Party loyalties aside. As he ran the hearings, he insisted that no rush to judgment be made on the part of the committee members. He stressed the importance of examining all the facts and determining if those facts translated into impeachable offenses. In the spirit of impartiality, Rodino, a Democrat and an Italian American, rejected making available to the public an audiotape in which the Republican president slighted Italian Americans.

During the final days of July, the committee concluded its hearings and voted to consent to three of four proposed articles of impeachment. Thanks in part to the fairness by which Rodino conducted the hearings, the vote extended beyond party lines as some Republicans joined Democrats in advocating impeachment.

Afterward Rodino spoke with compassion about the now former president's predicament, taking no pleasure in the fact that his committee voted for impeachment. Rodino came to believe that Nixon's presidency might have survived Watergate if only he had been honest with the American public and revealed all he knew about the affair.

When Jimmy Carter became the Democratic Party presidential nominee in 1976, he considered naming Rodino his running mate, but the congressman declined. He retired from the House of Representatives in 1989 and became a professor of constitutional law at New Jersey's Seton Hall University.

Peter W. Rodino Jr. presided over the House Judiciary Committee's hearings to determine whether President Nixon should be impeached.

CHRONOLOGY

November 5, 1968   Richard Nixon becomes the thirty-seventh U.S. president.

June 17, 1972   Five men are taken into custody while attempting to break into and bug the headquarters of the Democratic National Committee, located in the Watergate office complex in Washington, D.C.

June 19, 1972   The *Washington Post* reports that James W. McCord Jr., security director of CREEP, is one of the five Watergate burglars. John Mitchell, the head of CREEP, says he has no knowledge of the operation.

August 1, 1972   The *Washington Post* reports that a twenty-five-thousand-dollar check, seemingly meant for CREEP, had been deposited in the bank account of Bernard L. Barker, one of the five burglars.

September 15, 1972   Barker, McCord, G. Gordon Liddy, E. Howard Hunt, Virgilio Gonzalez, Eugenio Martinez, and Frank Sturgis are indicted by a federal grand jury for their participation in the break-in.

September 29, 1972   The *Washington Post* reports that John Mitchell managed a top secret fund employed by the Republicans to spy on Democratic political activity.

October 10, 1972   The *Washington Post* reports that the FBI uncovered sufficient evidence to link the Watergate break-in to President Nixon's reelection campaign.

November 7, 1972   President Nixon is reelected in a landslide.

January 30, 1973   McCord and Liddy are convicted of conspiracy, burglary, and wiretapping in connection with the Watergate break-in.

February 7, 1973   The U.S. Senate establishes the Senate Select Committee to Investigate Campaign Practices, which will investigate the Watergate affair.

May 18, 1973   The Senate Select Committee commences hearings. Archibald Cox is appointed the U.S. Justice Department's special prosecutor for Watergate.

June 3, 1973	John Dean, former White House counsel, reports to the Senate Select Committee that he had discussed a Watergate cover-up with Nixon on over thirty-five occasions.
July 18–August 9, 1973	Cox subpoenas the White House for secret Watergate-related documents and audiotapes. The president refuses to hand them over.
August 15, 1973	The president tells the American people that conversations between a president and his advisers need to be kept confidential as a matter of national security.
October 20, 1973	Nixon has Cox fired in what came to be known as the "Saturday Night Massacre."
November 21, 1973	The Senate Select Committee makes it known that an eighteen-and-a-half-minute gap exists on an audiotape of a conversation between Nixon and Haldeman, Nixon's former chief of staff.
December 7, 1973	The White House is unable to account for the gap.
February 6, 1974	The U.S. House of Representatives authorizes its Committee on the Judiciary to determine if adequate grounds exist to impeach Nixon.
April 30, 1974	The White House makes available to the Committee on the Judiciary over twelve hundred pages of edited transcripts of Nixon audiotape recordings. The committee demands the actual tapes.
July 24, 1974	The U.S. Supreme Court unanimously rules that the president must release additional audiotapes.
July 27–30, 1974	The Committee on the Judiciary votes to consent to three of four proposed articles of impeachment.
August 8, 1974	Nixon announces his resignation from office.
August 9, 1974	The president officially resigns and is replaced by Vice President Gerald Ford.
September 8, 1974	Ford pardons Nixon for all wrongdoing in the Watergate affair.

For Further Information

Books

Carl Bernstein and Bob Woodward, *All the President's Men*. New York: Simon and Schuster, 1974.

———, *The Final Days*. New York: Simon and Schuster, 1976.

Barbara Silberdick Feinberg, *Watergate: Scandal in the White House*. New York: Franklin Watts, 1990.

David K. Fremon, *The Watergate Scandal in American History*. Springfield, NJ: Enslow, 1998.

D.J. Herda, *United States v. Nixon: Watergate and the President*. Springfield, NJ: Enslow, 1996.

Pamela Kilian, *What Was Watergate?* New York: St. Martin's, 1990.

Rebecca Larsen, *Richard Nixon: Rise and Fall of a President*. New York: Franklin Watts, 1991.

Web Sites

Richard M. Nixon: The Watergate Tapes
www.lib.berkeley.edu/MRC/watergate.html
A Web site featuring transcripts and selections from President Nixon's White House audiotape recordings.

TIME Newsfile: Watergate
www.time.com/time/newsfiles/watergate
A Web site spotlighting a general history and analysis of Watergate, as reported in *Time* magazine.

Washington Post.com: Watergate
www.washingtonpost.com/wp-srv/national/longterm/watergate/front.htm
A Web site featuring a general history of Watergate, spotlighting *Washington Post* coverage of the affair.

Index

All the President's Men (Woodward and Bernstein), 34, 37
audiotape recordings, 5, 7–9, 19, 26, 30

Barker, Bernard L., 4, 12
Bernstein, Carl, 34
Butterfield, Alexander, 5, 38

Carter, Jimmy, 15
Central Intelligence Agency (CIA), 9, 33
Committee for the Reelection of the President (CREEP), 4, 15, 16, 25
Cox, Archibald, 5, 7, 38

Dean, John W., III, 16, 25, 33
Deep Throat, 37
Democratic National Campaign Committee, 4, 11

Ehrlichman, John D., 29
Ervin, Sam J., Jr., 41
executive privilege, 38

Federal Bureau of Investigation (FBI), 4, 33
Ford, Gerald, 9

Gonzalez, Virgilio, 12

Haldeman, H.R. "Bob," 9, 26
House of Representatives Committee on the Judiciary, 8, 9, 42
Hunt, E. Howard, 12

impeachment, 7–8, 9, 42
Internal Revenue Service (IRS), 29, 33

Kissinger, Henry, 9

Liddy, G. Gordon, 4–5, 15

Magruder, Jeb Stuart, 25
Martinez, Eugenio, 12
McCord, James W., Jr., 4–5, 16, 19
McGovern, George, 4
Mitchell, John, 4, 15, 25

Nixon, Richard, 4, 8–9, 20, 23, 25

Operation Gemstone, 15

plumbers, 4, 12, 15, 29

Republican National Committee, 16
Richardson, Elliot, 7, 38
Rodino, Peter W., Jr., 42
Ruckelshaus, William D., 7, 38

Saturday Night Massacre, 38
Senate Select Committee to Investigate Campaign Practices, 5, 25, 41
Sirica, John J., 16, 19
smoking gun, 20
Sturgis, Frank, 12
Supreme Court, 8, 19, 20

Washington Post (newspaper), 4, 16, 34
Watergate office complex, 4
Watergate tape 342, 30
White House Special Investigations Unit. *See* plumbers
Wills, Frank, 11
Woods, Rose Mary, 30
Woodward, Bob, 34

About the Author

Rob Edelman is a writer who lives with his wife, Audrey Kupferberg, in Amsterdam, New York. He has authored several books on baseball and movie and television personalities, and teaches film history at the University at Albany (SUNY). He enjoys watching old movies and attending baseball games.